THE OSTER ROASTER OVEN COOKBOOK

---

80 FOOLPROOF RECIPES TAILOR-MADE FOR YOUR KITCHEN'S MOST VERSATILE POT. | FOR BEGINNERS AND ADVANCED USERS.

PAMELA KENDRICK

CONTENTS

BEEF, PORK & LAMB

FISH & SEAFOOD

VEGETABLES & SIDE DISHES

DESSERTS

INTRODUCTION

The Oster roaster oven is one of the portable tabletop electrical cooking appliances available in the market. It is a multifunctional cooking appliance used to roast your favourite turkey, chicken, meat. It is also used for baking, steaming, warming, slow cooking and more. It consumes less electricity to work and gives 33 % faster cooking results compare with a convection oven. The oven comes with a 22 qt cooking capacity and capacity to cook a 26-pound turkey in a single cooking cycle. The Oster roasting oven comes with different kinds of accessories that help to make your cooking process easy. These accessories include a removable roasting pan, removable roasting rack and self-basting lid.

The Roaster oven temperature ranges between 150°F and 450°F which is ideal for cooking different types of foods. It saves your time, money, and stress instead of buying different cooking operations of each cooking operations. It also saves your kitchen countertop space. The body of the Oster oven is made up of stainless-steel material and removable steel pan makes this oven unique. It comes with an easily operate dial control system which helps to adjust the oven temperature and other settings. The self-basting feature gives the rid of hand basting method. The Oster roaster oven comes with a light indicator which helps when you preheat the oven. While preheating process the light indicator is in ON position and when the oven reaches its desire preheat temperature the light will automatically OFF.

The cookbook contains 80 tasty and delicious Oster roaster oven recipes that come from different categories like breakfast, poultry, beef, pork & seafood, vegetables & side dishes and desserts. All the recipes written in this cookbook are unique and written into an easily understandable form. The recipes are written with their preparation, cooking time, and step by step instructions. All the recipes written in this book are ends with their nutritional value information. The nutritional value information will help to keep track of daily calorie intake. Finally, the book contains a 30-days meal plan which helps to pre-plan your meal. This is the first book available in the market on this hot topic thanks for choosing my book. I hope you love and enjoy all the recipes written in this cookbook.

BREAKFAST

1

PERFECT POTATO CASSEROLE

Preparation Time: 10 minutes
Cooking Time: 35 minutes
Serve: 10
Ingredients:
•7 eggs
•8 oz cheddar cheese, grated
•20 oz frozen hash browns, diced
•1/2 cup milk
•1 onion, chopped & sautéed
•1 lb Italian sausage, cooked
•Pepper
•Salt
Directions:
1.Preheat the roaster oven to 350 F.
2.Spray roasting pan with cooking spray.
3.Add all ingredients into the large bowl and mix well.
4.Pour mixture into the prepared roasting pan.
5.Cover and bake for 35 minutes.
6.Serve and enjoy.
Nutritional Value (Amount per Serving):

- Calories 450
- Fat 30.8 g
- Carbohydrates 22.1 g
- Sugar 2.2 g
- Protein 2.6 g
- Cholesterol 177 mg

HASHBROWN CASSEROLE

Preparation Time: 10 minutes
Cooking Time: 35 minutes
Serve: 12
Ingredients:
•8 eggs
•16 oz curd cottage cheese
•6 oz Gruyere cheese, shredded
•8 oz cheddar cheese, shredded
•4 cups frozen hash browns, thawed
•1 onion, diced
•16 oz bacon, cooked & diced
•Pepper
•Salt
Directions:
1.Preheat the roaster oven to 350 F.
2.Spray roasting pan with cooking spray.
3.In a large mixing bowl, whisk eggs with pepper and salt.
4.Add remaining ingredients and mix well.
5.Pour mixture into the prepared roasting pan.
6.Cover and bake for 35 minutes.

7.Serve and enjoy.

Nutritional Value (Amount per Serving):

•Calories 556

•Fat 37.7 g

•Carbohydrates 21.9 g

•Sugar 2.9 g

•Protein 32 g

•Cholesterol 194 mg

TASTER TOT CASSEROLE

Preparation Time: 10 minutes
Cooking Time: 45 minutes
Serve: 8
Ingredients:
•8 eggs
•8 oz Colby Jack cheese, shredded
•2 green onions, chopped
•1/2 cup milk
•32 oz frozen tater tots
•1.25 lb bacon, cooked & chopped
•Pepper
•Salt
Directions:
1.Preheat the roaster oven to 350 F.
2.Spray roasting pan with cooking spray. Spread tater tots in a roasting pan.
3.In a bowl, whisk eggs with milk, pepper, and salt.
4.Add cheese, green onion, and bacon and stir well.
5.Pour egg mixture over tater tots.
6.Cover and bake for 45 minutes.

7.Serve and enjoy.

Nutritional Value (Amount per Serving):

•Calories 782
•Fat 54.1 g
•Carbohydrates 30.4 g
•Sugar 1.8 g
•Protein 41.1 g
•Cholesterol 268 mg

4

EASY BAKED OATMEAL

Preparation Time: 10 minutes
Cooking Time: 45 minutes
Serve: 9
Ingredients:
•2 eggs
•3 cups old-fashioned oats
•2 tsp vanilla
•1 tsp cinnamon
•1 1/2 tsp baking powder
•1/4 cup butter, melted
•1/2 cup brown sugar
•1 1/2 cups milk
•1/2 tsp salt
•For topping:
•1/4 cup butter, cubed
•1/4 cup brown sugar
•1/2 cup flour
Directions:
1.Preheat the roaster oven to 350 F.
2.Spray roasting pan with cooking spray.

3.In a mixing bowl, whisk eggs with vanilla, cinnamon, baking powder, butter, brown sugar, milk, and salt.

4.Add oats and stir until well combined.

5.Pour oats mixture into the roasting pan.

6.Mix together all topping ingredients and sprinkle over oat mixture.

7.Cover and bake for 40-45 minutes.

8.Serve and enjoy.

Nutritional Value (Amount per Serving):

•Calories 300

•Fat 13.9 g

•Carbohydrates 38 g

•Sugar 14.1 g

•Protein 6.9 g

•Cholesterol 67 mg

HEALTHY BREAKFAST CASSEROLE

Preparation Time: 10 minutes
Cooking Time: 35 minutes
Serve: 12
Ingredients:
- 6 eggs, lightly beaten
- 1 1/4 cup Swiss cheese, shredded
- 1 1/2 cups cottage cheese
- 2 cups cheddar cheese, shredded
- 4 cups shredded hash brown potatoes
- 1 onion, chopped & sauteed
- 1 lb bacon, cooked & chopped

Directions:
1. Preheat the roaster oven to 350 F.
2. Spray roasting pan with cooking spray.
3. Add all ingredients into the mixing bowl and mix until well combined.
4. Pour mixture into the roasting pan.
5. Cover and bake for 35 minutes.
6. Serve and enjoy.

Nutritional Value (Amount per Serving):

- •Calories 225
- •Fat 10.4 g
- •Carbohydrates 28.5 g
- •Sugar 10.5 g
- •Protein 5.2 g
- •Cholesterol 50 mg

DELICIOUS FRENCH EGGS

Preparation Time: 10 minutes
Cooking Time: 10 minutes
Serve: 6
Ingredients:
•6 large eggs
•1/4 cup heavy cream
•4 oz parmesan cheese, grated
•Pepper
•Salt
Directions:
1.Preheat the roaster oven to 425 F.
2.Place roasting rack in a toaster oven.
3.Spray 6-cups muffin pan with cooking spray.
4.Crack an egg into each cup. Drizzle each with 2 tsp of heavy cream. Season with pepper and salt.
5.Sprinkle each cup with 1 tablespoon of parmesan cheese.
6.Place muffin pan on roasting rack.
7.Cover and bake for 10-12 minutes.
8.Serve and enjoy.
Nutritional Value (Amount per Serving):

- •Calories 150
- •Fat 10.9 g
- •Carbohydrates 1.2 g
- •Sugar 0.4 g
- •Protein 12.5 g
- •Cholesterol 206 mg

VEGAN CARROT CAKE OATMEAL

Preparation Time: 10 minutes
Cooking Time: 50 minutes
Serve: 8
Ingredients:
- 1 flax egg
- 1 cup almond milk
- 2 tsp cinnamon
- 1/4 cup dates, chopped
- 1/4 cup shredded coconut
- 1/2 cup pecans, chopped
- 1 cup grated carrots
- 1/4 cup hemp seeds
- 1/4 cup vegan protein powder
- 1/4 cup maple syrup
- 1/2 cup applesauce
- 2 cups boiling water
- 2 cups rolled oats

Directions:
1. Preheat the roaster oven to 375 F.
2. Spray roasting pan with cooking spray.

3.Add boiling water and oats into the mixing bowl and let sit for 10-15 minutes.

4.Meanwhile, mix together the remaining ingredients into the mixing bowl. Add oats and mix well.

5.Pour oat mixture into the roasting pan.

6.Cover and bake for 50-60 minutes.

7.Serve and enjoy.

Nutritional Value (Amount per Serving):

•Calories 250

•Fat 12.4 g

•Carbohydrates 30.8 g

•Sugar 13.1 g

•Protein 6.5 g

•Cholesterol 23 mg

EASY BAKED FRITTATA

Preparation Time: 10 minutes
Cooking Time: 35 minutes
Serve: 12
Ingredients:
•12 eggs
•1 tsp garlic powder
•2 1/2 cups mushrooms, chopped
•1 cup cheddar cheese, shredded
•1 bell pepper, chopped
•1 small onion, chopped
•1 cup ham, chopped
•1 1/2 cups asparagus, chopped
•Pepper
•Salt
Directions:
1.Preheat the roaster oven to 375 F.
2.Spray roasting pan with cooking spray.
3.Add mushrooms, pepper, onion, ham, and asparagus into the roasting pan.

4.In a mixing bowl, whisk eggs with garlic powder, cheese, pepper, and salt.

5.Pour egg mixture over mushroom mixture.

6.Cover and bake for 30-35 minutes.

7.Serve and enjoy.

Nutritional Value (Amount per Serving):

•Calories 132

•Fat 8.6 g

•Carbohydrates 3.5 g

•Sugar 1.8 g

•Protein 10.8 g

•Cholesterol 180 mg

APPLE CINNAMON OATMEAL CUPS

Preparation Time: 10 minutes
Cooking Time: 20 minutes
Serve: 6
Ingredients:
- 1 egg
- 1 1/2 cups quick oats
- 1/2 apple, diced
- 2 tbsp honey
- 1/2 cup applesauce
- 1/2 cup milk
- 1 tsp cinnamon
- 3/4 tsp baking powder

Directions:
1. Preheat the roaster oven to 375 F.
2. Place roasting rack in a toaster oven.
3. Line 6-cups muffin pan with cupcake liners and set aside.
4. Add all ingredients into the mixing bowl and mix until well combined.
5. Spoon mixture into the prepared muffin cups.
6. Place muffin pan on roasting rack.

7.Cover and bake for 20 minutes.

8.Serve and enjoy.

Nutritional Value (Amount per Serving):

•Calories 139

•Fat 2.5 g

•Carbohydrates 26.2 g

•Sugar 10.9 g

•Protein 4.4 g

•Cholesterol 29 mg

HEALTHY CAULIFLOWER MUFFINS

Preparation Time: 10 minutes
Cooking Time: 20 minutes
Serve: 6
Ingredients:
- 1 1/2 cups cauliflower rice
- 3 eggs, lightly beaten
- 1/2 cup cheddar cheese
- 1/4 tsp garlic powder
- 1/4 cup onion, chopped
- 1/4 cup baby spinach, chopped
- 3 oz ham, diced
- Pepper
- Salt

Directions:
1. Preheat the roaster oven to 375 F.
2. Place roasting rack in a toaster oven.
3. Spray 6-cups muffin pan with cooking spray.
4. Add all ingredients into the bowl and mix until well combined.
5. Pour mixture into the prepared muffin pan.

6.Place muffin pan on roasting rack.

7.Cover and bake for 20 minutes.

8.Serve and enjoy.

Nutritional Value (Amount per Serving):

•Calories 109

•Fat 7 g

•Carbohydrates 3.1 g

•Sugar 1.5 g

•Protein 8.6 g

•Cholesterol 100 mg

POULTRY

11

CREAMY CHICKEN BREAST

Preparation Time: 10 minutes
Cooking Time: 60 minutes
Serve: 3
Ingredients:
- 3 chicken breasts, boneless
- 1 tsp garlic powder
- 1 tsp dried basil
- 1 tsp dried oregano
- 3/4 cup parmesan cheese, grated
- 1 cup sour cream
- 1 cup mozzarella cheese, shredded
- Pepper
- Salt

Directions:
1. Preheat the roaster oven to 375 F.
2. Place roasting rack in a roaster oven.
3. Spray baking dish with cooking spray.
4. Place chicken breasts into the baking dish and sprinkle with shredded mozzarella cheese.

5.In a bowl, mix sour cream, parmesan cheese, oregano, basil, garlic powder, pepper, and salt and pour over chicken.

6.Place baking dish on roasting rack.

7.Cover and bake for 60 minutes or until the internal temperature of the chicken reach 165 F.

8.Serve and enjoy.

Nutritional Value (Amount per Serving):

•Calories 537

•Fat 32.9 g

•Carbohydrates 5.4 g

•Sugar 0.4 g

•Protein 54 g

•Cholesterol 183 mg

BAKED CHICKEN WINGS

Preparation Time: 10 minutes
Cooking Time: 50 minutes
Serve: 4
Ingredients:
•1 lb chicken wings
•For rub:
•1/2 tbsp baking powder
•1/4 tsp Italian seasoning
•1/2 tsp ground paprika
•1/4 tsp garlic powder
•1/4 tsp pepper
•1/2 tsp salt
Directions:
1.Preheat the roaster oven to 375 F.
2.Place roasting rack in a roaster oven.
3.Mix together all rub ingredients and rub all over chicken wings.
4.Place chicken wings on a baking sheet.
5.Place baking sheet on roasting rack.

6.Cover and bake for 30 minutes. Flip chicken wings and bake for 20 minutes more.

7.Serve and enjoy.

Nutritional Value (Amount per Serving):

•Calories 220

•Fat 8.5 g

•Carbohydrates 1.3 g

•Sugar 0.1 g

•Protein 32.9 g

•Cholesterol 101 mg

13

TENDER & JUICY CHICKEN LEGS

Preparation Time: 10 minutes
Cooking Time: 40 minutes
Serve: 4
Ingredients:
•8 chicken drumsticks
•2 tbsp olive oil
For rub:
•1 tsp onion powder
•1/4 tsp chili powder
•1 1/2 tsp paprika
•1 tsp garlic powder
•1/2 tsp pepper
•1 tsp sea salt
Directions:
1.Preheat the roaster oven to 425 F.
2.Place roasting rack in a roaster oven.
3.In a small bowl, mix all rub ingredients.
4.Brush chicken drumsticks with oil and rub with spice mixture.
5.Place chicken drumsticks on the baking sheet.

6.Place baking sheet on roasting rack.

7.Cover and bake for 40-45 minutes.

8.Serve and enjoy.

Nutritional Value (Amount per Serving):

•Calories 223

•Fat 12.4 g

•Carbohydrates 1.7 g

•Sugar 0.5 g

•Protein 25.7 g

•Cholesterol 81 mg

14

JUICY BAKED CHICKEN BREAST

Preparation Time: 10 minutes
Cooking Time: 35 minutes
Serve: 4
Ingredients:
- 1 lb chicken breasts, boneless & skinless
- 1/2 tsp oregano
- 1/2 tsp garlic powder
- 1/2 tsp paprika
- 1/2 tbsp olive oil
- Pepper
- Salt

Directions:
1. Preheat the roaster oven to 375 F.
2. Place roasting rack in a roaster oven.
3. Place chicken breasts into the baking dish and drizzle with oil.
4. Sprinkle oregano, garlic powder, paprika, pepper, and salt over chicken.
5. Place baking dish on roasting rack.
6. Cover and bake for 25-35 minutes.

7.Serve and enjoy.

Nutritional Value (Amount per Serving):

•Calories 233

•Fat 1.2 g

•Carbohydrates 0.5 g

•Sugar 0.1 g

•Protein 32.9 g

•Cholesterol 101 mg

SALSA CHICKEN

Preparation Time: 10 minutes
Cooking Time: 25 minutes
Serve: 6
Ingredients:
•2 lbs chicken breasts, boneless & cut into pieces
•1 cup mozzarella cheese, shredded
•1/2 lime juice
•1/2 cilantro, chopped
•1/2 cup jalapeno, chopped
•1/2 cup onion, chopped
•2 cups tomatoes, chopped
•1/4 tsp red chili flakes
•1/4 tsp garlic powder
•1/4 tsp pepper
•1/4 tsp cumin
•1/2 tsp salt
Directions:
1.Preheat the roaster oven to 400 F.
2.Place roasting rack in a roaster oven.
3.In a mixing bowl, mix chicken, lime juice, cilantro, jalapeno,

onion, tomatoes, chili flakes, garlic powder, pepper, cumin, and salt.

4.Add chicken mixture into the baking dish and top with shredded cheese,

5.Place baking dish on roasting rack.

6.Cover and bake for 25-30 minutes.

7.Serve and enjoy.

Nutritional Value (Amount per Serving):

•Calories 320

•Fat 12.2 g

•Carbohydrates 4.4 g

•Sugar 2.4 g

•Protein 45.9 g

•Cholesterol 137 mg

16

FLAVORFUL BAKED CHICKEN

Preparation Time: 10 minutes
Cooking Time: 15 minutes
Serve: 4
Ingredients:
- 1 lb chicken breasts, boneless
- 1/4 tsp chili powder
- 1/4 tsp onion powder
- 1/4 tsp garlic powder
- 1 tbsp olive oil
- Pepper
- Salt

Directions:
1. Preheat the roaster oven to 450 F.
2. Place roasting rack in a roaster oven.
3. Place chicken breasts into the baking dish and drizzle with oil.
4. In a small bowl, mix chili powder, onion powder, garlic powder, pepper, and salt and sprinkle over chicken.
5. Place baking dish on roasting rack.
6. Cover and bake for 15-20 minutes.

7.Serve and enjoy.

Nutritional Value (Amount per Serving):

•Calories 247

•Fat 11.9 g

•Carbohydrates 0.4 g

•Sugar 0.1 g

•Protein 32.9 g

•Cholesterol 101 mg

BALSAMIC CHICKEN

Preparation Time: 10 minutes
Cooking Time: 25 minutes
Serve: 4
Ingredients:
•4 chicken breasts, boneless
•2 tsp dried oregano
•2 garlic cloves, minced
•1/2 cup balsamic vinegar
•2 tbsp soy sauce
•1/4 cup olive oil
•Pepper
•Salt
Directions:
1.Preheat the roaster oven to 400 F.
2.Place roasting rack in a roaster oven.
3.Place chicken breasts into the baking dish.
4.Mix together oil, soy sauce, vinegar, garlic, oregano, pepper, and salt and pour over chicken.
5.Place baking dish on roasting rack.
6.Cover and bake for 25 minutes.

7.Serve and enjoy.

Nutritional Value (Amount per Serving):

•Calories 401

•Fat 23.5 g

•Carbohydrates 1.9 g

•Sugar 0.3 g

•Protein 42.9 g

•Cholesterol 130 mg

18

SPICY CHICKEN BREAST

Preparation Time: 10 minutes
Cooking Time: 20 minutes
Serve: 4
Ingredients:
•2 chicken breasts, boneless
•2 tbsp butter, melted
•1 tbsp dried parsley
•1/4 tsp red chili flakes
•1/2 tsp pepper
•1/2 tsp chili powder
•1 tsp paprika
•1 tsp onion powder
•1 tsp garlic powder
•1 tsp salt
Directions:
1.Preheat the roaster oven to 450 F.
2.Place roasting rack in a roaster oven.
3.Place chicken breasts into the baking dish and drizzle with butter.

4.Mix together the remaining ingredients and sprinkle over the chicken.

5.Place baking dish on roasting rack.

6.Cover and bake for 20 minutes.

7.Serve and enjoy.

Nutritional Value (Amount per Serving):

•Calories 198

•Fat 11.3 g

•Carbohydrates 1.7 g

•Sugar 0.5 g

•Protein 21.5 g

•Cholesterol 80 mg

HEALTHY CHICKEN FAJITAS

Preparation Time: 10 minutes
Cooking Time: 30 minutes
Serve: 4
Ingredients:
•1 lb chicken breasts, boneless
•4 oz cheddar cheese, shredded
•1 onion, sliced
•1 bell pepper, sliced
•1/2 tbsp taco seasoning
Directions:
1.Preheat the roaster oven to 375 F.
2.Place roasting rack in a roaster oven.
3.Place chicken breasts into the baking dish.
4.Spread onion and bell pepper on top of chicken and sprinkle with taco seasoning. Sprinkle shredded cheese on top.
5.Place baking dish on roasting rack.
6.Cover and bake for 30-40 minutes.
7.Serve and enjoy.
Nutritional Value (Amount per Serving):
•Calories 350

- Fat 17.9 g
- Carbohydrates 5.2 g
- Sugar 2.8 g
- Protein 40.5 g
- Cholesterol 131 mg

20

ITALIAN CHICKEN

Preparation Time: 10 minutes
Cooking Time: 30 minutes
Serve: 4
Ingredients:
- 4 chicken breasts, boneless
- 1 cup mozzarella cheese, shredded
- 1/2 can artichoke hearts, sliced
- 1 cup cherry tomatoes, cut in half
- 1 zucchini, sliced
- 1 tbsp dried basil
- Pepper
- Salt

Directions:
1. Preheat the roaster oven to 375 F.
2. Place roasting rack in a roaster oven.
3. Place chicken breasts into the baking dish.
4. Add basil, zucchini, tomatoes, and artichoke hearts on top of chicken. Season with pepper and salt.
5. Sprinkle shredded cheese on top.
6. Place baking dish on roasting rack.

7.Cover and bake for 25-30 minutes.

8.Serve and enjoy.

Nutritional Value (Amount per Serving):

•Calories 323

•Fat 12.3 g

•Carbohydrates 5.8 g

•Sugar 2.2 g

•Protein 45.9 g

•Cholesterol 134 mg

21

BBQ PINEAPPLE CHICKEN

Preparation Time: 10 minutes
Cooking Time: 30 minutes
Serve: 4
Ingredients:
•4 chicken breasts, boneless
•2 green onions, diced
•1 cup mozzarella cheese, shredded
•1/4 cup onion, sliced
•6 bacon slices, cooked & diced
•1 cup pineapple, diced
•1 cup BBQ sauce
Directions:
1.Preheat the roaster oven to 375 F.
2.Place roasting rack in a roaster oven.
3.Place chicken breasts into the baking dish.
4.Pour BBQ sauce over chicken. Top with green onion, onion, bacon, and pineapple.
5.Sprinkle shredded cheese on top.
6.Place baking dish on roasting rack.
7.Cover and bake for 25-30 minutes.

8.Serve and enjoy.

Nutritional Value (Amount per Serving):
- Calories 571
- Fat 24.2 g
- Carbohydrates 30 g
- Sugar 20.8 g
- Protein 55.2 g
- Cholesterol 165 mg

22

BAKED CHICKEN THIGHS

Preparation Time: 10 minutes
Cooking Time: 30 minutes
Serve: 6
Ingredients:
•6 chicken thighs
•1 tbsp olive oil
•For rub:
•1 tsp garlic powder
•1 tsp onion powder
•1/2 tsp basil
•1/2 tsp oregano
•1/2 tsp pepper
•1/2 tsp salt
Directions:
1.Preheat the roaster oven to 400 F.
2.Place roasting rack in a roaster oven.
3.Brush chicken thighs with oil.
4.In a small bowl, mix all rub ingredients and rub all over the chicken thighs.
5.Place chicken thighs on a baking sheet.

6.Place baking sheet on roasting rack.

7.Cover and bake for 30-35 minutes.

8.Serve and enjoy.

Nutritional Value (Amount per Serving):

•Calories 301

•Fat 13.2 g

•Carbohydrates 0.9 g

•Sugar 0.3 g

•Protein 42.6 g

•Cholesterol 130 mg

23

CHEESY BROCCOLI CHICKEN

Preparation Time: 10 minutes
Cooking Time: 30 minutes
Serve: 4
Ingredients:
• 4 chicken breasts, skinless and boneless
• 1/2 cup ranch dressing
• 4 bacon slices, cooked and chopped
• 1 3/4 cups broccoli florets, blanched and chopped
• 1/3 cup mozzarella cheese, shredded
• 1 cup cheddar cheese, shredded
Directions:
1. Preheat the roaster oven to 375 F.
2. Place roasting rack in a roaster oven.
3. Add chicken into the baking dish and top with bacon and broccoli.
4. Pour ranch dressing over chicken and top with shredded cheese.
5. Place baking dish on roasting rack.
6. Cover and bake for 30 minutes.
7. Serve and enjoy.

Nutritional Value (Amount per Serving):
- Calories 523
- Fat 28.5 g
- Carbohydrates 5 g
- Sugar 1.6 g
- Protein 58.5 g
- Cholesterol 182 mg

24

HONEY MUSTARD CHICKEN

Preparation Time: 10 minutes
Cooking Time: 40 minutes
Serve: 6
Ingredients:
•6 chicken thighs
•1/2 cup honey
•1/4 cup yellow mustard
•Pepper
•Salt
Directions:
1.Preheat the roaster oven to 350 F.
2.Place roasting rack in a roaster oven.
3.Season chicken with pepper and salt and place into the baking dish.
4.Mix mustard and honey and pour over chicken.
5.Place baking dish on roasting rack.
6.Cover and bake for 40 minutes.
7.Serve and enjoy.
Nutritional Value (Amount per Serving):
•Calories 370

- •Fat 11.2 g
- •Carbohydrates 23.9 g
- •Sugar 23.3 g
- •Protein 42.8 g
- •Cholesterol 130 mg

25

MEATBALLS

Preparation Time: 10 minutes
Cooking Time: 25 minutes
Serve: 6
Ingredients:
•2 eggs, lightly beaten
•2 lbs ground chicken
•2 cups breadcrumbs
•1/2 cup milk
•1 tbsp garlic, minced
•1 onion, diced
•Pepper
•Salt
Directions:
1.Preheat the roaster oven to 400 F.
2.Place roasting rack in a roaster oven.
3.Line baking sheet with parchment paper and set aside.
4.Add all ingredients into the bowl and mix until well combined.
5.Make balls from the meat mixture and place them on a baking sheet.

6.Place baking sheet on roasting rack.

7.Cover and bake for 25 minutes.

8.Serve and enjoy.

Nutritional Value (Amount per Serving):

•Calories 470

•Fat 15 g

•Carbohydrates 29.2 g

•Sugar 4.1 g

•Protein 51.4 g

•Cholesterol 191 mg

26

DELICIOUS PESTO CHICKEN

Preparation Time: 10 minutes
Cooking Time: 25 minutes
Serve: 4
Ingredients:
•4 chicken breasts, boneless
•1/2 cup basil pesto
•1/2 cup mozzarella cheese, shredded
•Pepper
•Salt
Directions:
1.Preheat the roaster oven to 400 F.
2.Place roasting rack in a roaster oven.
3.Season chicken with pepper and salt and place into the baking dish.
4.Pour pesto and cheese over chicken.
5.Place baking dish on roasting rack.
6.Cover and bake for 25 minutes.
7.Serve and enjoy.
Nutritional Value (Amount per Serving):
•Calories 288

- •Fat 11.5 g
- •Carbohydrates 0.2 g
- •Sugar 0 g
- •Protein 43.3 g
- •Cholesterol 132 mg

27

CHEESY CHICKEN CASSEROLE

Preparation Time: 10 minutes
Cooking Time: 40 minutes
Serve: 8
Ingredients:
- 2 lbs cooked chicken, shredded
- 1 oz fresh lemon juice
- 1 tbsp Dijon mustard
- 5 oz ham, cut into small pieces
- 6 oz cream cheese, softened
- 4 oz butter, melted
- 5 oz Swiss cheese slices
- 1/2 tsp salt

Directions:
1. Preheat the roaster oven to 350 F.
2. Place roasting rack in a roaster oven.
3. Place chicken in the baking dish and top with ham.
4. Add butter, lemon juice, mustard, cream cheese, and salt into the blender and blend well and pour over chicken.
5. Arrange Swiss cheese slices on top of chicken.
6. Place baking dish on roasting rack.

7.Cover and bake for 40 minutes.

8.Serve and enjoy.

Nutritional Value (Amount per Serving):

•Calories 435

•Fat 27.8 g

•Carbohydrates 2.1 g

•Sugar 0.8 g

•Protein 42.7 g

•Cholesterol 164 mg

28

CHICKEN PATTIES

Preparation Time: 10 minutes
Cooking Time: 25 minutes
Serve: 4
Ingredients:
•1 egg, lightly beaten
•1 lb ground chicken
•1/8 tsp red pepper flakes
•2 garlic cloves, minced
•1/2 cup onion, minced
•3/4 cup breadcrumbs
•1 cup cheddar cheese, shredded
•1 cup carrot, grated
•1 cup cauliflower, grated
•Pepper
•Salt
Directions:
1.Preheat the roaster oven to 400 F.
2.Place roasting rack in a roaster oven.
3.Add all ingredients into the bowl and mix until well combined.

4.Make patties from the mixture and place them on a parchment-lined baking sheet.

5.Place baking sheet on roasting rack.

6.Cover and bake for 25 minutes.

7.Serve and enjoy.

Nutritional Value (Amount per Serving):

•Calories 451

•Fat 20 g

•Carbohydrates 20.9 g

•Sugar 4.1 g

•Protein 44.9 g

•Cholesterol 172 mg

29

BAKED CHICKEN TENDERS

Preparation Time: 10 minutes
Cooking Time: 30 minutes
Serve: 4
Ingredients:
- 2 lbs frozen chicken tenders
- 1/2 cup butter, melted
- 1 tsp garlic powder
- 1 tbsp paprika
- 1 tbsp dried oregano
- 1 cup parmesan cheese, grated
- Pepper
- Salt

Directions:
1. Preheat the roaster oven to 350 F.
2. Place roasting rack in a roaster oven.
3. In a shallow bowl, mix cheese, oregano, paprika, garlic powder, pepper, and salt.
4. Brush chicken tenders with melted butter and coat with cheese mixture.
5. Place chicken tenders on the baking sheet.

6.Place baking sheet on roasting rack.

7.Cover and bake for 30 minutes.

8.Serve and enjoy.

Nutritional Value (Amount per Serving):

•Calories 526

•Fat 30.6 g

•Carbohydrates 3.1 g

•Sugar 0.4 g

•Protein 57.6 g

•Cholesterol 196 mg

30

GREEK CHICKEN CASSEROLE

Preparation Time: 10 minutes
Cooking Time: 20 minutes
Serve: 4
Ingredients:
- 1 lb chicken breast, cooked & shredded
- 1/2 cup salsa
- 1 cup cheddar cheese, shredded
- 4 oz cream cheese, softened
- 4 cups cauliflower florets, cooked
- 1/4 cup Greek yogurt
- 1/8 tsp pepper
- 1/2 tsp kosher salt

Directions:
1. Preheat the roaster oven to 375 F.
2. Place roasting rack in a roaster oven.
3. In a large bowl, mix chicken, cauliflower, salsa, cream cheese, yogurt, pepper, and salt.
4. Pour chicken mixture into the baking dish and top with cheddar cheese.
5. Place baking dish on roasting rack.

6.Cover and bake for 20 minutes.

7.Serve and enjoy.

Nutritional Value (Amount per Serving):

•Calories 385

•Fat 22.5 g

•Carbohydrates 9 g

•Sugar 4.1 g

•Protein 37 g

•Cholesterol 134 mg

BEEF, PORK & LAMB

31

DELICIOUS PORK TENDERLOIN

Preparation Time: 10 minutes
Cooking Time: 30 minutes
Serve: 4
Ingredients:
- 1 lb pork tenderloin
- 1 1/2 cups olive oil
- 1 tsp pepper
- 1/4 cup brown sugar
- 1/4 cup lime juice
- 1/2 cup vinegar
- 4 cloves
- 1 tbsp ground allspice
- 3 shallots, chopped
- 4 pepperoncini, chopped
- 2 tbsp jalapeno peppers, chopped

Directions:
1.Preheat the roaster oven to 400 F.
2.Spray roasting pan with cooking spray.
3.Add all ingredients except meat into the blender and blend until smooth.

4.Place pork tenderloin in a large bowl. Pour blended mixture over pork tenderloin and marinate meat for 1 hour.

5.Place marinated pork tenderloin in a roasting pan.

6.Cover and bake for 20-30 minutes.

7.Serve and enjoy.

Nutritional Value (Amount per Serving):

•Calories 862

•Fat 79.8 g

•Carbohydrates 10.7 g

•Sugar 9 g

•Protein 29.9 g

•Cholesterol 83 mg

32

BEEF STEW

Preparation Time: 10 minutes
Cooking Time: 3 hours
Serve: 4
Ingredients:
•2 lbs beef chuck roast, boneless
•1.5 oz beef stew seasoning
•3 cups chicken stock
•20 oz can condense cream of tomato soup
•2 potatoes, cubed
•4 carrots, peel & slice
Directions:
1.Preheat the roaster oven to 250 F.
2.Spray roasting pan with cooking spray.
3.Add meat, potatoes, and carrots into the roasting pan.
4.Mix together remaining ingredients and pour over meat mixture.
5.Cover and cook for 3 hours.
6.Serve and enjoy.
Nutritional Value (Amount per Serving):
•Calories 961

- Fat 65.3 g
- Carbohydrates 40.6 g
- Sugar 13.7 g
- Protein 64.7 g
- Cholesterol 241 mg

33

JUICY PORK CHOPS

Preparation Time: 10 minutes
Cooking Time: 18 minutes
Serve: 4
Ingredients:
•4 pork chops, boneless
•2 tbsp olive oil
•1 tsp oregano
•1 tsp garlic powder
•1 tsp onion powder
•1 tbsp paprika
•Pepper
•Salt
Directions:
1.Preheat the roaster oven to 400 F.
2.Place roasting rack in a roaster oven.
3.In a small bowl, mix oregano, garlic powder, onion powder, paprika, pepper, and salt.
4.Brush pork chops with oil and rub with spice mixture.
5.Place pork chops in the baking dish.
6.Place baking dish on roasting rack.

7.Cover and bake for 18 minutes.

8.Serve and enjoy.

Nutritional Value (Amount per Serving):

•Calories 327

•Fat 27.2 g

•Carbohydrates 2.2 g

•Sugar 0.6 g

•Protein 18.5 g

•Cholesterol 69 mg

34
———

SPICY PORK BELLY

Preparation Time: 10 minutes
Cooking Time: 50 minutes
Serve: 6
Ingredients:
- 3 lbs pork belly, cut into 2-inch cubes
- 4 green onions, chopped
- 1 tbsp sesame seeds
- 1/4 tsp pepper
- 1 tbsp sesame oil
- 2 tbsp brown sugar
- 1/4 cup vinegar
- 1/4 cup soy sauce
- 1 tsp red chili flakes
- 2 garlic cloves, minced
- 1/4 tsp salt

Directions:
1. Add all ingredients except green onions and sesame seeds into the mixing bowl and mix well and marinate for 1 hour.
2. Preheat the roaster oven to 400 F.
3. Place roasting rack in a roaster oven.

4.Place marinated pork belly pieces on a baking sheet.

5.Place baking sheet on roasting rack.

6.Cover and bake for 30 minutes. Turn pork belly pieces and bake for 20 minutes more.

7.Garnish with green onion and sesame seeds.

8.Serve and enjoy.

Nutritional Value (Amount per Serving):

•Calories 998

•Fat 93.1 g

•Carbohydrates 8.2 g

•Sugar 3.4 g

•Protein 29.8 g

•Cholesterol 154 mg

35

TENDER & JUICY PORK CHOPS

Preparation Time: 10 minutes
Cooking Time: 20 minutes
Serve: 4
Ingredients:
•4 pork chops, boneless
•2 tbsp olive oil
•For rub:
•1/2 tsp Italian seasoning
•1 tsp paprika
•1/2 tsp garlic powder
•2 tbsp brown sugar
•1/4 tsp pepper
•1/2 tsp sea salt
Directions:
1.Preheat the roaster oven to 375 F.
2.Place roasting rack in a roaster oven.
3.In a small bowl, mix all rub ingredients.
4.Brush pork chops with oil and rub with spice mixture.
5.Place pork chops on the baking sheet.
6.Place baking sheet on roasting rack.

7.Cover and bake for 20-25 minutes.

8.Serve and enjoy.

Nutritional Value (Amount per Serving):

•Calories 338

•Fat 27.4 g

•Carbohydrates 5.1 g

•Sugar 4.6 g

•Protein 18.1 g

•Cholesterol 69 mg

36

EASY PORK RIBS

Preparation Time: 10 minutes
Cooking Time: 30 minutes
Serve: 8
Ingredients:
•2 lbs pork ribs, boneless
•1 tbsp onion powder
•1 1/2 tbsp garlic powder
•1 tbsp olive oil
•Pepper
•Salt
Directions:
1.Preheat the roaster oven to 350 F.
2.Place roasting rack in a roaster oven.
3.Brush pork ribs with oil and rub with onion powder, garlic powder, pepper, and salt.
4.Place pork ribs on a baking sheet.
5.Place baking sheet on roasting rack.
6.Cover and bake for 25-30 minutes.
7.Serve and enjoy.
Nutritional Value (Amount per Serving):

PAMELA KENDRICK

- Calories 333
- Fat 21.9 g
- Carbohydrates 1.9 g
- Sugar 0.7 g
- Protein 30.4 g
- Cholesterol 117mg

37

BAKED LAMB CHOPS

Preparation Time: 10 minutes
Cooking Time: 15 minutes
Serve: 4
Ingredients:
•8 lamb loin chops
•For rub:
•2 tsp dried herb de Provence
• 1 tsp garlic, minced
•2 tbsp olive oil
•2 tbsp Dijon mustard
•Pepper
•Salt
Directions:
1.Preheat the roaster oven to 425 F.
2.Place roasting rack in a roaster oven.
3.Mix together all rub ingredients and rub all over lamb chops.
4.Place lamb chops in the baking dish.
5.Place baking dish on roasting rack.
6.Cover and bake for 15 minutes.

7.Serve and enjoy.

Nutritional Value (Amount per Serving):

•Calories 67
•Fat 7.4 g
•Carbohydrates 0.7 g
•Sugar 0.1 g
•Protein 0.4 g
•Cholesterol 0 mg

38

BAKED LAMB KEBABS

Preparation Time: 10 minutes
Cooking Time: 35 minutes
Serve: 8
Ingredients:
•2 1/2 lbs ground lamb
•1/8 tsp ground coriander
•1/8 tsp ground cumin
•1/8 tsp pepper
•1 onion, chopped
•1 1/2 tsp salt
Directions:
1.Preheat the roaster oven to 375 F.
2.Place roasting rack in a roaster oven.
3.Add all ingredients into the mixing bowl and mix until well combined.
4.Make kebabs from the meat mixture and place them on a baking sheet.
5.Place baking sheet on roasting rack.
6.Cover and bake for 25-35 minutes.
7.Serve and enjoy.

Nutritional Value (Amount per Serving):
- Calories 269
- Fat 10.4 g
- Carbohydrates 1.3 g
- Sugar 0.6 g
- Protein 40 g
- Cholesterol 128 mg

39

MEATBALLS

Preparation Time: 10 minutes
Cooking Time: 20 minutes
Serve: 6
Ingredients:
- 2 lbs ground beef
- 1 egg, lightly beaten
- 1 tsp oregano
- 1 tsp garlic, minced
- 1 small onion, grated
- 1 tbsp fresh mint, chopped
- 1/4 cup fresh parsley, minced
- 1/2 tsp allspice
- 1 tsp paprika
- 1 tsp cinnamon
- 2 tsp cumin
- 2 tsp coriander
- Pepper
- Salt

Directions:
1. Preheat the roaster oven to 400 F.

2.Place roasting rack in a roaster oven.

3.Add all ingredients into the large bowl and mix until well combined.

4.Make balls from the meat mixture and place them on a baking sheet.

5.Place baking sheet on roasting rack.

6.Cover and bake for 20 minutes.

7.Serve and enjoy.

Nutritional Value (Amount per Serving):

•Calories 304

•Fat 10.4 g

•Carbohydrates 2.7 g

•Sugar 10.7 g

•Protein 47.3 g

•Cholesterol 162 mg

40

FLAVORFUL LAMB PATTIES

Preparation Time: 10 minutes
Cooking Time: 8 minutes
Serve: 4
Ingredients:
- 1 lb ground lamb
- 1 cup feta cheese, crumbled
- 1 tbsp garlic, minced
- 1/2 tsp chili powder
- 5 basil leaves, minced
- 10 mint leaves, minced
- 1/4 tsp pepper
- 1/4 cup fresh parsley, chopped
- 1 tsp dried oregano
- 1/2 tsp kosher salt

Directions:
1. Preheat the roaster oven to 400 F.
2. Place roasting rack in a roaster oven.
3. Add all ingredients into the mixing bowl and mix until well combined.

4.Make patties from the meat mixture and place them on a baking sheet.

5.Place baking sheet on roasting rack.

6.Cover and bake for 8 minutes.

7.Serve and enjoy.

Nutritional Value (Amount per Serving):

•Calories 331

•Fat 15 g

•Carbohydrates 5.4 g

•Sugar 1.7 g

•Protein 38.5 g

•Cholesterol 135 mg

41

TASTY SIRLOIN STEAK

Preparation Time: 10 minutes
Cooking Time: 30 minutes
Serve: 6
Ingredients:
•2 lbs sirloin steak, cut into 1-inch cubes
•1/4 cup olive oil
•2 cups fresh parsley, chopped
•1 tsp dried oregano
•1/2 tsp pepper
•2 garlic cloves, minced
•3 tbsp fresh lemon juice
•1/4 cup water
•1 tsp salt
Directions:
1.Preheat the roaster oven to 400 F.
2.Place roasting rack in a roaster oven.
3.Add all ingredients except beef into the large bowl and mix well.
4.Pour bowl mixture into the large zip-lock bag.

5.Add beef to the bag and shake well and place it in the fridge for 1 hour.

6.Place marinated beef on a baking sheet.

7.Place baking sheet on roasting rack.

8.Cover and bake for 30 minutes.

9.Serve and enjoy.

Nutritional Value (Amount per Serving):

•Calories 366

•Fat 18 g

•Carbohydrates 2 g

•Sugar 0.4 g

•Protein 46.6 g

•Cholesterol 135 mg

42

DELICIOUS MEATLOAF

Preparation Time: 10 minutes
Cooking Time: 20 minutes
Serve: 4
Ingredients:
- 1 lb ground pork
- 1/4 tsp garlic powder
- 1 egg, lightly beaten
- 3 tbsp breadcrumbs
- 1 onion, chopped
- Pepper
- Salt

Directions:
1. Preheat the roaster oven to 400 F.
2. Place roasting rack in a roaster oven.
3. Spray a loaf pan with cooking spray and set aside.
4. Add all ingredients into the mixing bowl and mix until well combined.
5. Pour meat mixture into the loaf pan.
6. Place loaf pan on roasting rack.
7. Cover and bake for 20 minutes.

8.Serve and enjoy.

Nutritional Value (Amount per Serving):

•Calories 210

•Fat 5.4 g

•Carbohydrates 6.9 g

•Sugar 1.6 g

•Protein 32.1 g

•Cholesterol 124 mg

43

MEATBALLS

Preparation Time: 10 minutes
Cooking Time: 12 minutes
Serve: 4
Ingredients:
- 1 egg, lightly beaten
- 4 oz ground lamb meat
- 1/2 tbsp lemon zest
- 1 tbsp oregano, chopped
- Pepper
- Salt

Directions:
1. Preheat the roaster oven to 400 F.
2. Place roasting rack in a roaster oven.
3. Line baking tray with parchment paper and set aside.
4. Add all ingredients into the bowl and mix until well combined.
5. Make balls from the meat mixture and place them on a baking sheet.
6. Place baking sheet on roasting rack.
7. Cover and bake for 12 minutes.

8.Serve and enjoy.

Nutritional Value (Amount per Serving):

•Calories 75

•Fat 5 g

•Carbohydrates 1 g

•Sugar 0.2 g

•Protein 6.8 g

•Cholesterol 61 mg

44

BAKED PATTIES

Preparation Time: 10 minutes
Cooking Time: 15 minutes
Serve: 6
Ingredients:
- 2 lbs ground beef
- 1 tsp onion powder
- 1 tsp garlic powder
- 1 cup mozzarella cheese, grated
- 1/4 tsp chili powder
- Pepper
- Salt

Directions:
1. Preheat the roaster oven to 400 F.
2. Place roasting rack in a roaster oven.
3. Add all ingredients into the large bowl and mix until well combined.
4. Make patties from the meat mixture and place them on a baking sheet.
5. Place baking sheet on roasting rack.
6. Cover and bake for 15 minutes.

7.Serve and enjoy.

Nutritional Value (Amount per Serving):
- Calories 295
- Fat 10.3 g
- Carbohydrates 0.8 g
- Sugar 0.3 g
- Protein 47.3 g
- Cholesterol 138 mg

45

FLAVORFUL LAMB CHOPS

Preparation Time: 10 minutes
Cooking Time: 30 minutes
Serve: 4
Ingredients:
• 4 lamb chops
• 1 tsp garlic powder
• 1 tsp ground cinnamon
• 1 1/2 tsp tarragon
• 1 1/2 tsp ginger
• 1/4 cup brown sugar
• Pepper
• Salt
Directions:
1. Preheat the roaster oven to 375 F.
2. Place roasting rack in a roaster oven.
3. Add garlic powder, cinnamon, tarragon, ginger, brown sugar, pepper, and salt into the zip-lock bag and mix well.
4. Add lamb chops in a zip-lock bag. Seal bag and place in the refrigerator for 2 hours.
5. Place marinated lamb chops on a baking sheet.

6.Place baking sheet on roasting rack.

7.Cover and bake for 30 minutes.

8.Serve and enjoy.

Nutritional Value (Amount per Serving):

•Calories 651

•Fat 24.1 g

•Carbohydrates 10.5 g

•Sugar 9 g

•Protein 92.1 g

•Cholesterol 294 mg

46

EASY RANCH PORK CHOPS

Preparation Time: 10 minutes
Cooking Time: 35 minutes
Serve: 6
Ingredients:
•6 pork chops, boneless
•1 tsp dried parsley
•1 oz ranch seasoning
•2 tbsp olive oil
Directions:
1.Preheat the roaster oven to 390 F.
2.Place roasting rack in a roaster oven.
3.Mix oil, dried parsley, and ranch seasoning and rub over pork chops.
4.Place pork chops on a baking sheet.
5.Place baking sheet on roasting rack.
6.Cover and bake for 35 minutes.
7.Serve and enjoy.
Nutritional Value (Amount per Serving):
•Calories 310

- Fat 24.6 g
- Carbohydrates 0 g
- Sugar 0 g
- Protein 18 g
- Cholesterol 69 mg

47

ROSEMARY PORK CHOPS

Preparation Time: 10 minutes
Cooking Time: 30 minutes
Serve: 4
Ingredients:
•4 pork chops, boneless
•1 tbsp fresh rosemary, chopped
•1/4 tsp pepper
•3 garlic cloves, minced
•1/4 tsp salt
Directions:
1.Preheat the roaster oven to 350 F.
2.Place roasting rack in a roaster oven.
3.Season pork chops with pepper and salt and set aside.
4.In a small bowl, mix together garlic and rosemary and rub over pork chops.
5.Place pork chops on the baking sheet.
6.Place baking sheet on roasting rack.
7.Cover and bake for 30 minutes.
8.Serve and enjoy.
Nutritional Value (Amount per Serving):

- •Calories 265
- •Fat 20.1 g
- •Carbohydrates 1.5 g
- •Sugar 0 g
- •Protein 18.2 g
- •Cholesterol 69 mg

48

BAKED PORK TENDERLOIN

Preparation Time: 10 minutes
Cooking Time: 20 minutes
Serve: 6
Ingredients:
- 2 lbs pork tenderloin
- 1 tbsp garlic, minced
- 1 tsp dried oregano
- 1 tbsp olive oil
- 1/4 cup honey
- 1/4 cup soy sauce
- Pepper
- Salt

Directions:
1. Preheat the roaster oven to 350 F.
2. Place roasting rack in a roaster oven.
3. Add honey and soy sauce into the small saucepan and cook over medium heat until reduced by half.
4. Mix garlic, oregano, pepper, and salt and rub all over pork tenderloin.
5. Heat oil in a large pan over medium heat.

6.Cook tenderloin on each side for 2 minutes.

7.Place pork tenderloin onto the baking sheet and brush with honey mixture.

8.Place baking sheet on roasting rack.

9.Cover and bake for 20 minutes.

10. Serve and enjoy.

Nutritional Value (Amount per Serving):

•Calories 285

•Fat 7.7 g

•Carbohydrates 13.1 g

•Sugar 11.8 g

•Protein 40.4 g

•Cholesterol 110 mg

FISH & SEAFOOD

49

BAKED CATFISH FILLETS

Preparation Time: 10 minutes
Cooking Time: 15 minutes
Serve: 4
Ingredients:
- 1 lb catfish fillets
- 1 tsp red chili flakes
- 1/2 tsp chili powder
- 1/2 tsp ground cumin
- 1 tbsp dried oregano, crushed
- 1 tsp onion powder
- Pepper
- Salt

Directions:
1. Preheat the roaster oven to 350 F.
2. Place roasting rack in a roaster oven.
3. In a small bowl, mix cumin, chili powder, chili flakes, onion powder, oregano, pepper, and salt and rub over fish fillets.
4. Place fish fillets into the baking dish.
5. Place baking dish on roasting rack.
6. Cover and bake for 15 minutes.

7.Serve and enjoy.

Nutritional Value (Amount per Serving):

•Calories 165

•Fat 9 g

•Carbohydrates 2 g

•Sugar 0.5 g

•Protein 19 g

•Cholesterol 55 mg

50

BAKED CAJUN COD

Preparation Time: 10 minutes
Cooking Time: 15 minutes
Serve: 6
Ingredients:
•3 cod fillets, cut in half
•1 tbsp olive oil
•1/4 cup butter, melted
•1 tbsp Cajun seasoning
•1 tbsp garlic, minced
•Pepper
•Salt
Directions:
1.Preheat the roaster oven to 400 F.
2.Place roasting rack in a roaster oven.
3.Season fish fillets with pepper and salt and place them in a baking dish.
4.Mix together the remaining ingredients and pour over fish fillets.
5.Place baking dish on roasting rack.
6.Cover and bake for 15 minutes.

7.Serve and enjoy.

Nutritional Value (Amount per Serving):

•Calories 125

•Fat 10.4 g

•Carbohydrates 0.5 g

•Sugar 0 g

•Protein 8.2 g

•Cholesterol 42 mg

51

PARMESAN RED SNAPPER

Preparation Time: 10 minutes
Cooking Time: 12 minutes
Serve: 2
Ingredients:
•8 oz red snapper fillets
•1/2 tsp Cajun seasoning
•1/4 tsp Worcestershire sauce
•1 garlic clove, minced
•1/4 cup butter
•2 tbsp parmesan cheese, grated
•1/4 cup breadcrumbs
Directions:
1.Preheat the roaster oven to 400 F.
2.Place roasting rack in a roaster oven.
3.Melt butter in a pan over low heat.
4.Add Cajun seasoning, garlic, and Worcestershire sauce into the melted butter and stir well.
5.Brush fish fillets with melted butter and place into the baking dish.
6.Mix cheese and breadcrumbs and sprinkle over fish fillets.

7.Place baking dish on roasting rack.

8.Cover and bake for 12 minutes.

9.Serve and enjoy.

Nutritional Value (Amount per Serving):

•Calories 425

•Fat 27 g

•Carbohydrates 10.6 g

•Sugar 1 g

•Protein 33.9 g

•Cholesterol 119 mg

52

ASIAN HADDOCK

Preparation Time: 10 minutes
Cooking Time: 25 minutes
Serve: 2
Ingredients:
- 1 lb haddock fillets
- 1/4 cup onion, diced
- 1 tsp ginger, grated
- 3/4 cup soy sauce
- 1/4 cup parsley, chopped
- 1 lemon juice
- 1/4 cup brown sugar
- Pepper
- Salt

Directions:
1. Preheat the roaster oven to 325 F.
2. Place roasting rack in a roaster oven.
3. Add fish fillets and remaining ingredients into the large bowl and coat well and place in the fridge for 1 hour.
4. Place marinated fish fillets into the baking dish.
5. Place baking dish on roasting rack.

6.Cover and bake for 25 minutes.

7.Serve and enjoy.

Nutritional Value (Amount per Serving):

•Calories 390

•Fat 2.5 g

•Carbohydrates 28 g

•Sugar 20.4 g

•Protein 61.7 g

•Cholesterol 168 mg

53

LEMON PEPPER BASA

Preparation Time: 10 minutes
Cooking Time: 10 minutes
Serve: 4
Ingredients:
•4 basa fish fillets
•1/4 tsp lemon pepper seasoning
•4 tbsp fresh lemon juice
•8 tsp butter, melted
•1/2 tsp garlic powder
•Salt
Directions:
1.Preheat the roaster oven to 425 F.
2.Place roasting rack in a roaster oven.
3.Place fish fillets into the baking dish.
4.Pour remaining ingredients over fish fillets.
5.Place baking dish on roasting rack.
6.Cover and bake for 10 minutes.
7.Serve and enjoy.
Nutritional Value (Amount per Serving):
•Calories 215

- Fat 15.3 g
- Carbohydrates 3.8 g
- Sugar 2.3 g
- Protein 15.4 g
- Cholesterol 20 mg

54

EASY SHRIMP CASSEROLE

Preparation Time: 10 minutes
Cooking Time: 30 minutes
Serve: 10
Ingredients:
- 1 lb shrimp, peeled & tail off
- 2 tsp onion powder
- 10.5 oz can cream of mushroom soup
- 12 oz rice
- 2 tsp old bay seasoning
- 2 cups cheddar cheese, shredded
- 1 tsp salt

Directions:
1. Preheat the roaster oven to 350 F.
2. Place roasting rack in a roaster oven.
3. Cook rice according to the packet instructions.
4. Add shrimp into the boiling water and cook for 5 minutes. Drain well.
5. In a bowl, mix rice, shrimp, and remaining ingredients and pour into the greased baking dish.
6. Place baking dish on roasting rack.

7.Cover and bake for 30 minutes.

8.Serve and enjoy.

Nutritional Value (Amount per Serving):

•Calories 285

•Fat 9 g

•Carbohydrates 31 g

•Sugar 1 g

•Protein 18.8 g

•Cholesterol 120 mg

55

BAKED BLACKENED SHRIMP

Preparation Time: 10 minutes
Cooking Time: 10 minutes
Serve: 6
Ingredients:
- 1 lb shrimp, deveined
- 2 tsp blackened seasoning
- 1 tbsp olive oil
- 1/4 tsp pepper
- 1/4 tsp salt

Directions:
1. Preheat the roaster oven to 400 F.
2. Place roasting rack in a roaster oven.
3. Toss shrimp with oil, pepper, blackened seasoning, and salt.
4. Transfer shrimp into the baking dish.
5. Place baking dish on roasting rack.
6. Cover and bake for 10 minutes.
7. Serve and enjoy.

Nutritional Value (Amount per Serving):
- Calories 165

- Fat 4.3 g
- Carbohydrates 10.5 g
- Sugar 0 g
- Protein 20.6 g
- Cholesterol 159 mg

56

SPICY SHRIMP

Preparation Time: 10 minutes
Cooking Time: 8 minutes
Serve: 4
Ingredients:
- 2 lbs shrimp, peeled & deveined
- 1/4 tsp cayenne pepper
- 2 tbsp chili powder
- 2 tbsp olive oil
- 1 tsp kosher salt

Directions:
1. Preheat the roaster oven to 400 F.
2. Place roasting rack in a roaster oven.
3. Toss shrimp with remaining ingredients.
4. Transfer shrimp into the baking dish.
5. Place baking dish on roasting rack.
6. Cover and bake for 8 minutes.
7. Serve and enjoy.

Nutritional Value (Amount per Serving):
- Calories 345

- Fat 11.5 g
- Carbohydrates 6.1 g
- Sugar 0.5 g
- Protein 52.3 g
- Cholesterol 478 mg

57

BAKED WHITE FISH FILLET

Preparation Time: 10 minutes
Cooking Time: 15 minutes
Serve: 4
Ingredients:
•1 lb white fish fillets
•2 tbsp garlic, minced
•2 tbsp olive oil
•2 tbsp dried parsley
•1/4 tsp red chili flakes
•Pepper
•Salt
Directions:
1.Preheat the roaster oven to 400 F.
2.Place roasting rack in a roaster oven.
3.Place fish fillets in a baking dish and drizzle with oil.
4.Sprinkle with chili flakes, parsley, and garlic. Season with pepper and salt.
5.Place baking dish on roasting rack.
6.Cover and bake for 15 minutes.
7.Serve and enjoy.

Nutritional Value (Amount per Serving):
- Calories 265
- Fat 15.6 g
- Carbohydrates 1.5 g
- Sugar 0.1 g
- Protein 28.1 g
- Cholesterol 87 mg

58

FLAVORS HERB SALMON

Preparation Time: 10 minutes
Cooking Time: 15 minutes
Serve: 4
Ingredients:
- 1 lb salmon fillets
- 1/4 tsp dried basil
- 1/4 tsp dried thyme
- 1/2 tbsp dried rosemary
- 1 tbsp olive oil
- Pepper
- Salt

Directions:
1. Preheat the roaster oven to 400 F.
2. Place roasting rack in a roaster oven.
3. Place salmon skin-side down on the baking sheet.
4. Mix olive oil, thyme, basil, and rosemary in a small bowl.
5. Brush salmon with oil mixture.
6. Place baking sheet on roasting rack.
7. Cover and bake for 15 minutes.
8. Serve and enjoy.

Nutritional Value (Amount per Serving):
- Calories 185
- Fat 10.6 g
- Carbohydrates 0.4 g
- Sugar 0 g
- Protein 22.1 g
- Cholesterol 50 mg

VEGETABLES & SIDE DISHES

59

STUFFED PEPPERS

Preparation Time: 10 minutes
Cooking Time: 25 minutes
Serve: 6
Ingredients:
- 3 bell peppers, cut in half & remove seeds
- 1/4 cup feta cheese, crumbled
- 1/2 cup cherry tomatoes, sliced
- 2 garlic cloves, minced
- 1 1/2 cups cooked quinoa
- 1/3 cup chickpeas, rinsed
- 1/2 tsp oregano
- 1/2 tsp salt

Directions:
1. Preheat the roaster oven to 400 F.
2. Place roasting rack in a roaster oven.
3. In a bowl, mix quinoa, tomatoes, chickpeas, oregano, garlic, and salt.
4. Stuff quinoa mixture into the bell pepper halves and place on a baking sheet.
5. Place baking sheet on roasting rack.

6.Cover and bake for 25 minutes.

7.Top peppers with crumbled cheese and serve.

Nutritional Value (Amount per Serving):

•Calories 237

•Fat 4.8 g

•Carbohydrates 39.8 g

•Sugar 4.9 g

•Protein 9.8 g

•Cholesterol 6 mg

60

ZUCCHINI CASSEROLE

Preparation Time: 10 minutes
Cooking Time: 45 minutes
Serve: 6
Ingredients:
- 2 egg whites
- 1/4 cup parmesan cheese, grated
- 1/4 cup feta cheese, crumbled
- 2 small yellow squash, diced
- 2 small zucchini, diced
- 1 tsp dried basil
- 1/2 tsp pepper
- 2 tsp garlic powder
- 1/4 cup breadcrumbs
- 3 cups baby spinach
- 2 tbsp olive oil
- 1/2 tsp kosher salt

Directions:
1. Preheat the roaster oven to 400 F.
2. Place roasting rack in a roaster oven.
3. Spray a baking dish with cooking spray and set aside.

4.Heat oil in a pan over medium heat.

5.Add squash, zucchini, and spinach and sauté for 5 minutes or until spinach is wilted.

6.Transfer squash mixture into the large bowl.

7.Add remaining ingredients to the bowl and mix well.

8.Spread mixture into the prepared baking dish.

9.Place baking dish on roasting rack.

10. Cover and bake for 30-40 minutes.

11. Serve and enjoy.

Nutritional Value (Amount per Serving):

•Calories 113

•Fat 7.4 g

•Carbohydrates 7.7 g

•Sugar 2.3 g

•Protein 5.6 g

•Cholesterol 9 mg

61

Baked Carrots
    Preparation Time: 10 minutes
    Cooking Time: 20 minutes
    Serve: 6
    Ingredients:
    •2 lbs carrots, peel & cut into fries shape
    •2 tbsp olive oil
    •For spice:
    •2 tsp dried basil
    •1 tsp dried rosemary
    •3 tsp dried parsley
    •1/4 tsp chili flakes
    •2 tsp dried oregano
    •1 tsp salt
    Directions:
    1.Preheat the roaster oven to 400 F.
    2.Place roasting rack in a roaster oven.
    3.Add allspice ingredients into the bowl.
    4.Add carrots and oil and toss well to coat.
    5.Transfer carrots onto the baking sheet.

6.Place baking sheet on roasting rack.

7.Cover and bake for 20 minutes.

8.Serve and enjoy.

Nutritional Value (Amount per Serving):

•Calories 104

•Fat 4.8 g

•Carbohydrates 15.4 g

•Sugar 7.5 g

•Protein 1.3 g

•Cholesterol 0 mg

62

BAKED GARLIC POTATOES

Preparation Time: 10 minutes
Cooking Time: 25 minutes
Serve: 4
Ingredients:
- 1 lb baby potatoes, cut into pieces
- 1 tsp thyme, chopped
- 2 garlic cloves, minced
- 1 tbsp olive oil
- 1 tbsp parsley, chopped
- 1/8 cup feta cheese, crumbled
- Pepper
- Salt

Directions:
1. Preheat the roaster oven to 400 F.
2. Place roasting rack in a roaster oven.
3. Toss potatoes with thyme, garlic, oil, pepper, and salt.
4. Spread potatoes onto the baking sheet.
5. Place baking sheet on roasting rack.
6. Cover and bake for 20-25 minutes.
7. Top with feta cheese and serve.

Nutritional Value (Amount per Serving):
- Calories 112
- Fat 4.7 g
- Carbohydrates 15 g
- Sugar 0.2 g
- Protein 3.7 g
- Cholesterol 4 mg

63

BAKED BUTTERNUT SQUASH

Preparation Time: 10 minutes
Cooking Time: 40 minutes
Serve: 4
Ingredients:
•3 lbs butternut squash, peeled, seeded, and cut into 1-inch cubes
•1 1/2 tbsp olive oil
•1/2 tsp cinnamon
•1 1/2 tbsp honey
•Pepper
•Salt
Directions:
1.Preheat the roaster oven to 400 F.
2.Place roasting rack in a roaster oven.
3.In a bowl, toss squash cubes with the remaining ingredients.
4.Spread squash cubes on a baking sheet.
5.Place baking sheet on roasting rack.
6.Cover and bake for 35-40 minutes.
7.Serve and enjoy.
Nutritional Value (Amount per Serving):

- •Calories 220
- •Fat 5.6 g
- •Carbohydrates 45.1 g
- •Sugar 12 g
- •Protein 3.4 g
- •Cholesterol 0 mg

64

BAKED SWEET POTATOES

Preparation Time: 10 minutes
Cooking Time: 40 minutes
Serve: 4
Ingredients:
- 2 large sweet potatoes, cut into 1-inch cubes
- 3/4 tsp paprika
- 1 tbsp olive oil
- 1/4 tsp onion powder
- 1/2 tsp garlic powder
- 1/2 tsp cumin
- 1/2 tsp chili powder
- 1/4 tsp pepper
- 1/2 tsp salt

Directions:
1. Preheat the roaster oven to 400 F.
2. Place roasting rack in a roaster oven.
3. Line baking sheet with parchment paper and set aside.
4. In a bowl, toss sweet potatoes with remaining ingredients until well coated.
5. Spread sweet potatoes on a baking sheet.

6.Place baking sheet on roasting rack.

7.Cover and bake for 40 minutes.

8.Serve and enjoy.

Nutritional Value (Amount per Serving):

•Calories 95

•Fat 3.8 g

•Carbohydrates 14.9 g

•Sugar 0.5 g

•Protein 1 g

•Cholesterol 0 mg

VEGETABLE CASSEROLE

Preparation Time: 10 minutes
Cooking Time: 1 hour 15 minutes
Serve: 12
Ingredients:
- 16 oz frozen broccoli, thawed
- 8 oz can water chestnuts, drained and sliced
- 10.5 oz cream of mushroom soup
- 8 oz mozzarella cheese, grated
- 16 oz frozen cauliflower, thawed
- 8 oz can bean sprouts, drained
- 8 oz cheddar cheese, grated
- 2 eggs, lightly beaten
- 1 onion, diced
- 1 cup mayonnaise
- Pepper
- Salt

Directions:
1. Preheat the roaster oven to 350 F.
2. Place roasting rack in a roaster oven.
3. Spray a baking dish with cooking spray and set aside.

4.In a mixing bowl, mix together mayonnaise, onions, eggs, soup, pepper, and salt.

5.Add broccoli, cauliflower, water chestnuts, and bean sprouts into the baking dish.

6.Pour mayonnaise mixture over vegetable mixture.

7.Sprinkle cheese on top.

8.Place baking dish on roasting rack.

9.Cover and bake for 1 hour 15 minutes.

10. Serve and enjoy.

Nutritional Value (Amount per Serving):

•Calories 260

•Fat 17.8 g

•Carbohydrates 13.2 g

•Sugar 4.5 g

•Protein 14 g

•Cholesterol 62 mg

66

BAKED POTATO CASSEROLE

Preparation Time: 10 minutes
Cooking Time: 60 minutes
Serve: 6
Ingredients:
- 2 eggs
- 1 cup cheddar cheese, shredded
- 10 potatoes, peeled and halved
- 3 tbsp butter
- 1 cup sour cream
- 8 oz cream cheese, softened
- Pepper
- Salt

Directions:
1. Preheat the roaster oven to 325 F.
2. Place roasting rack in a roaster oven.
3. Spray a baking dish with cooking spray and set aside.
4. Add potatoes to the boiling water and boil for 10 minutes. Drain well and place in a mixing bowl.
5. Mash the potatoes using masher until smooth.

6.Add remaining ingredients into the mashed potatoes and stir well to combine.

7.Pour potato mixture into the baking dish.

8.Place baking dish on roasting rack.

9.Cover and bake for 50 minutes.

10. Serve and enjoy.

Nutritional Value (Amount per Serving):

•Calories 605

•Fat 35 g

•Carbohydrates 58 g

•Sugar 4.4 g

•Protein 16.6 g

•Cholesterol 148 mg

67

SQUASH ZUCCHINI TOMATO BAKE

Preparation Time: 10 minutes
Cooking Time: 30 minutes
Serve: 6
Ingredients:
•3 tomatoes, sliced
•3/4 cup parmesan cheese, shredded
•2 yellow squash, sliced
•2 medium zucchinis, sliced
•1 tbsp olive oil
•Pepper
•Salt
Directions:
1.Preheat the roaster oven to 350 F.
2.Place roasting rack in a roaster oven.
3.Spray a baking dish with cooking spray and set aside.
4.Arrange sliced tomatoes, squash, and zucchinis alternately in the baking dish.
5.Drizzle with oil and season with pepper and salt.
6.Sprinkle parmesan cheese on top of vegetables.
7.Place baking dish on roasting rack.

8.Cover and bake for 30 minutes.

9.Serve and enjoy.

Nutritional Value (Amount per Serving):

•Calories 85

•Fat 5 g

•Carbohydrates 5.5 g

•Sugar 3.1 g

•Protein 4.9 g

•Cholesterol 8 mg

68

PARMESAN SQUASH CASSEROLE

Preparation Time: 10 minutes
Cooking Time: 45 minutes
Serve: 4
Ingredients:
•4 medium squash, cut into slices
•1 medium onion, sliced
•1/4 cup parmesan cheese, shredded
•3/4 stick butter, cut into cubes
•Pepper
•Salt
Directions:
1.Preheat the roaster oven to 350 F.
2.Place roasting rack in a roaster oven.
3.Spray a baking dish with cooking spray and set aside.
4.Layer squash slices, onion, butter, pepper, and salt in a prepared baking dish and sprinkle with cheese.
5.Place baking dish on roasting rack.
6.Cover and bake for 45 minutes.
7.Serve and enjoy.
Nutritional Value (Amount per Serving):

- •Calories 215
- •Fat 18.8 g
- •Carbohydrates 9.4 g
- •Sugar 4.6 g
- •Protein 4.7 g
- •Cholesterol 50 mg

69

BAKED BROCCOLI & BRUSSELS SPROUT

Preparation Time: 10 minutes
Cooking Time: 30 minutes
Serve: 6
Ingredients:
- 1 lb broccoli, cut into florets
- 1 lb Brussels sprouts, cut ends
- 1 tsp paprika
- 1 tsp garlic powder
- 1/2 tsp pepper
- 3 tbsp olive oil
- 1/2 onion, chopped
- 3/4 tsp salt

Directions:
1. Preheat the roaster oven to 390 F.
2. Place roasting rack in a roaster oven.
3. Add all ingredients into the bowl and toss well.
4. Then spread the vegetable mixture on a baking sheet.
5. Place baking sheet on roasting rack.
6. Cover and bake for 30 minutes.
7. Serve and enjoy.

Nutritional Value (Amount per Serving):
- Calories 124
- Fat 7.6 g
- Carbohydrates 13.4 g
- Sugar 3.5 g
- Protein 5 g
- Cholesterol 0 mg

70

BAKED POTATO WEDGES

Preparation Time: 10 minutes
Cooking Time: 15 minutes
Serve: 4
Ingredients:
•2 medium potatoes, cut into wedges
•1/2 tsp paprika
•1 1/2 tbsp olive oil
•1/4 tsp pepper
•1/8 tsp cayenne pepper
•1/4 tsp garlic powder
•1 tsp sea salt
Directions:
1.Preheat the roaster oven to 400 F.
2.Place roasting rack in a roaster oven.
3.Soak potato wedges into the water for 30 minutes. Drain well and pat dry.
4.In a bowl, toss potato wedges with the remaining ingredients.
5.Spread potato wedges on a baking sheet.
6.Place baking sheet on roasting rack.

7.Cover and bake for 15 minutes.

8.Serve and enjoy.

Nutritional Value (Amount per Serving):

•Calories 122

•Fat 5.4 g

•Carbohydrates 17.1 g

•Sugar 1.3 g

•Protein 1.9 g

•Cholesterol 0 mg

71

BAKED CHICKEN DIP

Preparation Time: 10 minutes
Cooking Time: 25 minutes
Serve: 8
Ingredients:
- 2 chicken breasts, skinless, boneless, cooked and shredded
- 1/4 cup blue cheese, crumbled
- 1/2 cup ranch dressing
- 1/2 cup hot sauce
- 8 oz cream cheese, softened
- 1 cup Monterey jack cheese, shredded
- 1 cup cheddar cheese, shredded

Directions:
1. Preheat the roaster oven to 350 F.
2. Place roasting rack in a roaster oven.
3. Spray a baking dish with cooking spray and set aside.
4. Add cream cheese into the baking dish and top with shredded chicken, ranch dressing, and hot sauce.
5. Sprinkle cheddar cheese, Monterey jack cheese, and blue cheese on top of chicken mixture.
6. Place baking dish on roasting rack.

7.Cover and bake for 25 minutes.

8.Serve and enjoy.

Nutritional Value (Amount per Serving):

•Calories 295

•Fat 22.8 g

•Carbohydrates 2 g

•Sugar 0.6 g

•Protein 20.8 g

•Cholesterol 94 mg

72

SPICY CHEESE DIP

Preparation Time: 10 minutes
Cooking Time: 30 minutes
Serve: 10
Ingredients:
- 16 oz cream cheese, softened
- 1 cup sour cream
- 1/2 cup salsa
- 3 cups cheddar cheese, shredded

Directions:
1. Preheat the roaster oven to 350 F.
2. Place roasting rack in a roaster oven.
3. Spray a baking dish with cooking spray and set aside.
4. In a bowl, mix together all ingredients until well combined and pour into the baking dish.
5. Place baking dish on roasting rack.
6. Cover and bake for 30 minutes.
7. Serve and enjoy.

Nutritional Value (Amount per Serving):
- Calories 345

- Fat 31.9 g
- Carbohydrates 3.4 g
- Sugar 0.7 g
- Protein 12.8 g
- Cholesterol 96 mg

DESSERTS

73

POUND CAKE

Preparation Time: 10 minutes
Cooking Time: 55 minutes
Serve: 10
Ingredients:
•4 eggs
•1/4 cup cream cheese
•1/4 cup butter
•1 tsp baking powder
•1 tbsp coconut flour
•1 cup almond flour
•1/2 cup sour cream
•1 tsp vanilla
•1 cup monk fruit sweetener
Directions:
1.Preheat the roaster oven to 350 F.
2.Place roasting rack in a roaster oven.
3.The grease cake pan and set aside.
4.In a bowl, mix together almond flour, baking powder, and coconut flour.
5.In a separate bowl, add cream cheese and butter and

microwave for 30 seconds. Stir well and microwave for 3o seconds more.

6.Stir in sour cream, vanilla, and sweetener.

7.Pour cream cheese mixture into the almond flour mixture and stir to combine.

8.Add eggs in batter one by one and stir to combine.

9.Pour batter into the prepared cake pan.

10. Place cake pan on roasting rack.

11. Cover and bake for 55 minutes.

12. Serve and enjoy.

Nutritional Value (Amount per Serving):

•Calories 210

•Fat 16.9 g

•Carbohydrates 8.3 g

•Sugar 5.5 g

•Protein 3.2 g

•Cholesterol 89 mg

74

LEMON CAKE

Preparation Time: 10 minutes
Cooking Time: 60 minutes
Serve: 16
Ingredients:
- 6 eggs
- 1/3 cup erythritol
- 4 oz cream cheese, softened
- 1 cup butter, softened
- 2 tsp xanthan gum
- 2 cups almond flour
- 2 egg yolks
- 2 tsp lemon extract

Directions:
1. Preheat the roaster oven to 325 F.
2. Place roasting rack in a roaster oven.
3. Grease loaf pan and set aside.
4. In a bowl, mix together almond flour and xanthan gum and set aside.
5. In a large bowl, beat cream cheese and butter until smooth.

6.Add sweetener and lemon extract and beat until the mixture becomes fluffy.

7.Add eggs and egg yolk one by one and beat until combined.

8.Add almond flour mixture and beat until just combined.

9.Pour batter into the prepared loaf pan.

10. Place loaf pan on roasting rack.

11. Cover and bake for 60 minutes.

12. Serve and enjoy.

Nutritional Value (Amount per Serving):
- •Calories 250
- •Fat 23.7 g
- •Carbohydrates 3.2 g
- •Sugar 0.7 g
- •Protein 3.1 g
- •Cholesterol 126 mg

75

CHOCOLATE CAKE

Preparation Time: 10 minutes
Cooking Time: 14 minutes
Serve: 8
Ingredients:
•3 eggs
•1/3 cup milk
•2 1/4 tsp baking powder
•1/4 cup cocoa powder
•1 1/2 cups almond flour
•1 1/2 tsp vanilla
•1/3 cup erythritol
•Pinch of salt
Directions:
1.Preheat the roaster oven to 350 F.
2.Place roasting rack in a roaster oven.
3.Grease an 8-inch cake pan and set aside.
4.Add all ingredients into the mixing bowl and mix until well combined.
5.Pour batter into the prepared cake pan.
6.Place cake pan on roasting rack.

7.Cover and bake for 14 minutes.

8.Serve and enjoy.

Nutritional Value (Amount per Serving):

•Calories 190

•Fat 15.7 g

•Carbohydrates 6.7 g

•Sugar 1.4 g

•Protein 2.8 g

•Cholesterol 61 mg

76

FUDGEY BROWNIES

Preparation Time: 10 minutes
Cooking Time: 15 minutes
Serve: 16
Ingredients:
- 4 eggs
- 1/2 cup cocoa powder
- 1 cup creamy almond butter
- 2 scoops whey protein powder
- 1/3 cup Swerve
- 2 tbsp coconut flour
- Pinch of salt

Directions:
1. Preheat the roaster oven to 325 F.
2. Place roasting rack in a toaster oven.
3. Line baking pan with parchment paper and set aside.
4. In a small bowl, mix together protein powder, cocoa powder, coconut flour, and salt.
5. Add eggs, sweetener, and almond butter into the stand mixer and mix until fluffy.

6.Slowly add protein powder mixture to egg mixture and mix until smooth.

7.Pour batter into the prepared pan.

8.Place baking pan on roasting rack.

9.Cover and bake for 15 minutes.

10. Serve and enjoy.

Nutritional Value (Amount per Serving):

•Calories 135

•Fat 10.3 g

•Carbohydrates 6.1 g

•Sugar 1.8 g

•Protein 7.8 g

•Cholesterol 49 mg

77

BROWNIE MUFFINS

Preparation Time: 10 minutes
Cooking Time: 15 minutes
Serve: 6
Ingredients:
•3 eggs
•1 tbsp gelatin
•1/2 cup Swerve
•1 cup almond flour
•1/3 cup butter, melted
•1/3 cup cocoa powder
Directions:
1.Preheat the roaster oven to 350 F.
2.Place roasting rack in a roaster oven.
3.Line 6-cups muffin pan with cupcake liners and set aside.
4.Add all ingredients into the mixing bowl and stir until well combined.
5.Pour mixture into the muffin pan.
6.Place muffin pan on roasting rack.
7.Cover and bake for 15 minutes.
8.Serve and enjoy.

Nutritional Value (Amount per Serving):
- Calories 255
- Fat 23.1 g
- Carbohydrates 6.3 g
- Sugar 0.9 g
- Protein 4.8 g
- Cholesterol 109 mg

78

BAKED PEARS

Preparation Time: 10 minutes
Cooking Time: 25 minutes
Serve: 4
Ingredients:
•4 pears, cut in half & core
•1/4 tsp cinnamon
•1/2 cup maple syrup
•1 tsp vanilla
Directions:
1.Preheat the roaster oven to 375 F.
2.Place roasting rack in a roaster oven.
3.Line baking sheet with parchment paper and set aside.
4.Arrange pears on the prepared baking sheet and sprinkle with cinnamon.
5.In a small bowl, mix maple syrup and vanilla and drizzle over pears.
6.Place baking sheet on roasting rack.
7.Cover and bake for 25 minutes.
8.Serve and enjoy.
Nutritional Value (Amount per Serving):

- •Calories 75
- •Fat 5.6 g
- •Carbohydrates 5 g
- •Sugar 0.7 g
- •Protein 2.8 g
- •Cholesterol 41 mg

79

CHOCOLATE MUFFINS

Preparation Time: 10 minutes
Cooking Time: 30 minutes
Serve: 6
Ingredients:
- 2 eggs
- 1/8 tsp vanilla
- 1/4 tsp cinnamon
- 1/4 cup Swerve
- 1/4 cup cocoa powder
- 1/3 cup coconut flour
- 2 tbsp coconut oil
- 1/2 tsp baking powder
- 1 cup grated zucchini
- 1/2 tsp baking soda
- 1/8 tsp salt

Directions:
1. Preheat the roaster oven to 350 F.
2. Place roasting rack in a roaster oven.
3. Line 6-cups muffin pan with cupcake liners and set aside.

4.Add all ingredients into the food processor and process until just combined.

5.Spoon mixture into the muffin cups.

6.Place muffin pan on roasting rack.

7.Cover and bake for 25-30 minutes.

8.Serve and enjoy.

Nutritional Value (Amount per Serving):

•Calories 75

•Fat 5.6 g

•Carbohydrates 5 g

•Sugar 0.7 g

•Protein 2.8 g

•Cholesterol 41 mg

80

PUMPKIN MUFFINS

Preparation Time: 10 minutes
Cooking Time: 20 minutes
Serve: 6
Ingredients:
•2 eggs
•1 tbsp pumpkin spice
•1 1/2 cups almond flour
•1/4 tsp liquid stevia
•8 tbsp butter, melted
•1 tsp baking powder
•3 tbsp Swerve
•1 tbsp coconut flour
•Pinch of salt
Directions:
1.Preheat the roaster oven to 300 F.
2.Place roasting rack in a roaster oven.
3.Line 6-cups muffin pan with cupcake liners and set aside.
4.In a bowl, whisk together eggs, butter, and sweetener until combined.
5.Add remaining ingredients and stir until well combined.

6.Pour mixture into the muffin cups.

7.Spoon mixture into the muffin cups.

8.Place muffin pan on roasting rack.

9.Cover and bake for 15-20 minutes.

10. Serve and enjoy.

Nutritional Value (Amount per Serving):

•Calories 295

•Fat 27.5 g

•Carbohydrates 6.7 g

•Sugar 1.1 g

•Protein 1.9 g

•Cholesterol 82 mg

30-DAY MEAL PLAN

Day 1
    Breakfast- Perfect Potato Casserole
    Lunch- Creamy Chicken Breast
    Dinner- Lemon Pepper Basa
Day 2
    Breakfast- Hashbrown Casserole
    Lunch- Baked Chicken Wings
    Dinner- Asian Haddock
Day 3
    Breakfast- Taster Tot Casserole
    Lunch- Creamy Chicken Breast
    Dinner- Parmesan Red Snapper
Day 4
    Breakfast- Easy Baked Oatmeal
    Lunch- Baked Chicken Wings
    Dinner- Easy Ranch Pork Chops
Day 5
    Breakfast- Healthy Breakfast Casserole
    Lunch- Tender & Juicy Chicken Legs
    Dinner- Baked Cajun Cod

Day 6

Breakfast- Hashbrown Casserole

Lunch- Tender & Juicy Chicken Legs

Dinner- Baked Catfish Fillets

Day 7

Breakfast- Delicious French Eggs

Lunch- Juicy Baked Chicken Breast

Dinner- Baked Pork Tenderloin

Day 8

Breakfast- Vegan Carrot Cake Oatmeal

Lunch- Juicy Baked Chicken Breast

Dinner- Rosemary Pork Chops

Day 9

Breakfast- Easy Baked Frittata

Lunch- Flavorful Baked Chicken

Dinner- Hashbrown Casserole

Day 10

Breakfast- Apple Cinnamon Oatmeal Cups

Lunch- Salsa Chicken

Dinner- Easy Ranch Pork Chops

Day 11

Breakfast- Hashbrown Casserole

Lunch- Balsamic Chicken

Dinner- Flavorful Lamb Chops

Day 12

Breakfast- Easy Baked Oatmeal

Lunch- Balsamic Chicken

Dinner- Tasty Sirloin Steak

Day 13

Breakfast- Healthy Cauliflower Muffins

Lunch- Spicy Chicken Breast

Dinner- Baked Lamb Chops

Day 14

Breakfast- Apple Cinnamon Oatmeal Cups

Lunch- Healthy Chicken Fajitas

Dinner- Easy Pork Ribs

Day 15
Breakfast- Healthy Cauliflower Muffins
Lunch- Italian Chicken
Dinner- BBQ Pineapple Chicken
Day 16
Breakfast- Perfect Potato Casserole
Lunch- Creamy Chicken Breast
Dinner- Lemon Pepper Basa
Day 17
Breakfast- Hashbrown Casserole
Lunch- Baked Chicken Wings
Dinner- Asian Haddock
Day 18
Breakfast- Taster Tot Casserole
Lunch- Creamy Chicken Breast
Dinner- Parmesan Red Snapper
Day 19
Breakfast- Easy Baked Oatmeal
Lunch- Baked Chicken Wings
Dinner- Easy Ranch Pork Chops
Day 20
Breakfast- Healthy Breakfast Casserole
Lunch- Tender & Juicy Chicken Legs
Dinner- Baked Cajun Cod
Day 21
Breakfast- Hashbrown Casserole
Lunch- Tender & Juicy Chicken Legs
Dinner- Baked Catfish Fillets
Day 22
Breakfast- Delicious French Eggs
Lunch- Juicy Baked Chicken Breast
Dinner- Baked Pork Tenderloin
Day 23
Breakfast- Vegan Carrot Cake Oatmeal
Lunch- Juicy Baked Chicken Breast
Dinner- Rosemary Pork Chops

Day 24
Breakfast- Easy Baked Frittata
Lunch- Flavorful Baked Chicken
Dinner- Hashbrown Casserole
Day 25
Breakfast- Apple Cinnamon Oatmeal Cups
Lunch- Salsa Chicken
Dinner- Easy Ranch Pork Chops
Day 26
Breakfast- Hashbrown Casserole
Lunch- Balsamic Chicken
Dinner- Flavorful Lamb Chops
Day 27
Breakfast- Easy Baked Oatmeal
Lunch- Balsamic Chicken
Dinner- Tasty Sirloin Steak
Day 28
Breakfast- Healthy Cauliflower Muffins
Lunch- Spicy Chicken Breast
Dinner- Baked Lamb Chops
Day 29
Breakfast- Apple Cinnamon Oatmeal Cups
Lunch- Healthy Chicken Fajitas
Dinner- Easy Pork Ribs
Day 30
Breakfast- Healthy Cauliflower Muffins
Lunch- Italian Chicken
Dinner- BBQ Pineapple Chicken

CONCLUSION

The Oster roaster oven is one of the portable tabletop electrical cooking appliances available in the market. It is a multifunctional cooking appliance used to roast your favorite turkey, chicken, meat. It is also used for baking, steaming, warming, slow cooking and more. It consumes less electricity to work and gives 33 % faster cooking results compare with a convection oven.

The cookbook contains 80 tasty and delicious Oster roaster oven recipes that come from different categories like breakfast, poultry, beef, pork & seafood, vegetables & side dishes and desserts. All the recipes written in this cookbook are unique and written into an easily understandable form. The recipes are written with their preparation, cooking time, and step by step instructions. All the recipes written in this book are ends with their nutritional value information.

CPSIA information can be obtained
at www.ICGtesting.com
Printed in the USA
BVHW042247211121
622215BV00004B/50